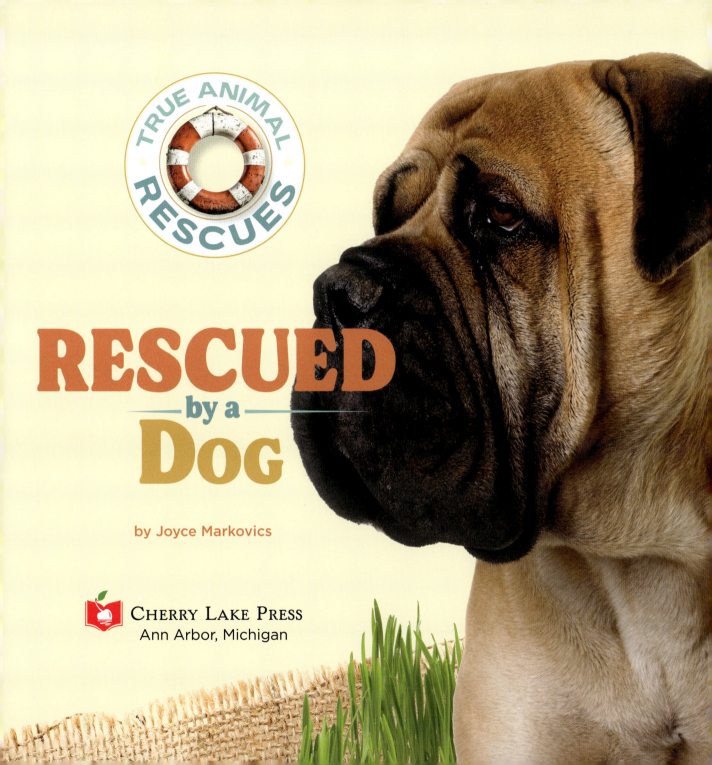

True Animal Rescues

RESCUED by a Dog

by Joyce Markovics

Cherry Lake Press
Ann Arbor, Michigan

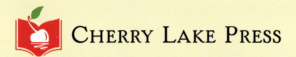

Published in the United States of America by Cherry Lake Publishing
Ann Arbor, Michigan
www.cherrylakepublishing.com

Reading Adviser: Beth Walker Gambro, MS Ed., Reading Consultant, Yorkville, IL

Book Designer: Ed Morgan
Book Developer: Bowerbird Books

Photo Credits: © Streamlight Studios/Shutterstock, cover; freepik.com, title page and table of contents; © HokieTim/Shutterstock, 4–5; © nivasinjeti12/Shutterstock, 6; freepik.com, 7; Courtesy of Gabby Bannon, 8 and 11; freepik.com, 9; © Thichaa/Shutterstock, 10; freepik.com, 12; © Jeremy Christensen/Shutterstock, 13; freepik.com, 14–15; © Halfpoint/Shutterstock, 17; freepik.com, 18–19, 21.

Copyright © 2026 by Cherry Lake Publishing Group

All rights reserved. No part of this book may be reproduced or utilized in any form or by any means without written permission from the publisher.

Cherry Lake Press is an imprint of Cherry Lake Publishing Group.

Library of Congress Cataloging-in-Publication Data has been filed and is available at catalog.loc.gov.

Printed in the United States of America

Note from publisher: Websites change regularly, and their future contents are outside of our control. Supervise children when conducting any recommended online searches for extended learning opportunities.

Contents

Rusty to the Rescue	4
Hero Dog Ella	12
Sarah Saves the Day	16
Tater Tot and Tom	20
Profile: Dog Rescuers	22
Glossary	23
Find Out More	24
Index	24
About the Author	24

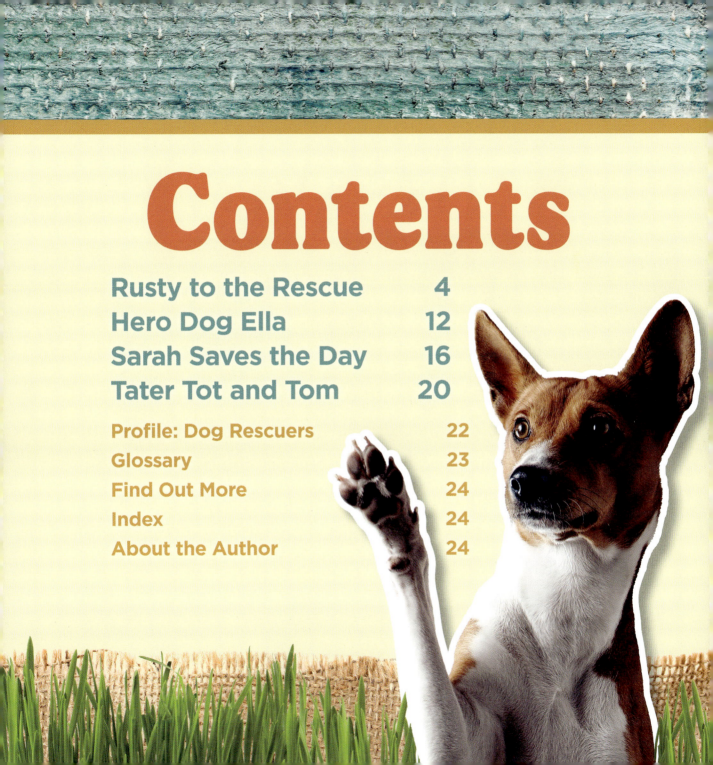

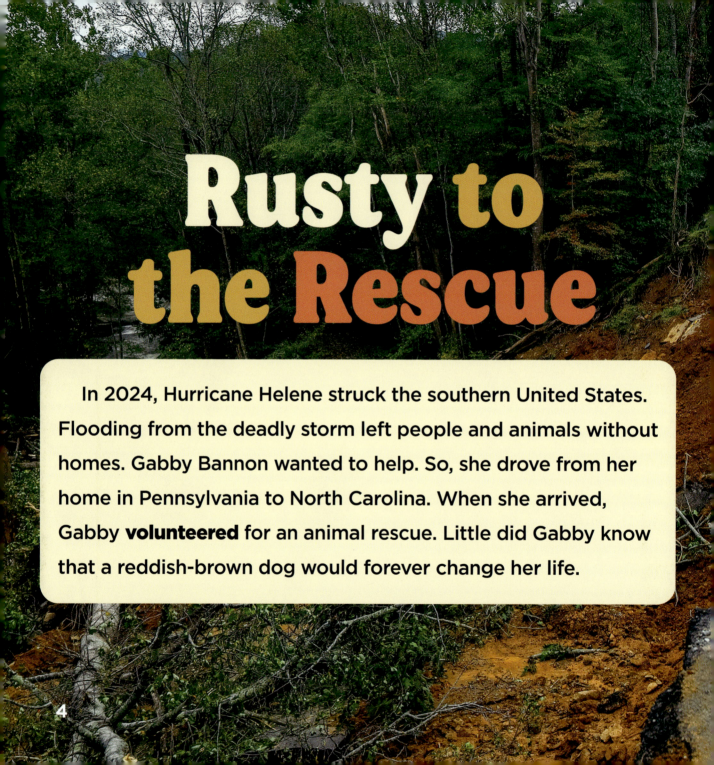

Rusty to the Rescue

In 2024, Hurricane Helene struck the southern United States. Flooding from the deadly storm left people and animals without homes. Gabby Bannon wanted to help. So, she drove from her home in Pennsylvania to North Carolina. When she arrived, Gabby **volunteered** for an animal rescue. Little did Gabby know that a reddish-brown dog would forever change her life.

Hurricane Helene affected several states, including North and South Carolina, Georgia, and Florida. It caused billions of dollars in damage.

Volunteers spotted the dog, known as Rusty. He was wandering around a town in North Carolina. "He was brought into the **shelter**," Gabby said. Right away, she sensed something special about the dog. "When I put a leash on Rusty . . . I felt this instant connection," said Gabby. "I can't really explain why, but he seemed to have a gentle soul."

Dogs, like these, often form bonds with other dogs. Rusty was found with another dog near an apartment building.

A few days later, Gabby drove Rusty and some other dogs back to Pennsylvania. There, they would be **adopted**. The dogs were put in crates for the long trip. But 3-year-old Rusty was afraid. So, Gabby let him ride up front.

"When I arrived home 11 hours later, I knew he would be with us," said Gabby. Right away, Rusty felt like a family member. Gabby's two young children loved him. "He blended right in and adores the kids," said Gabby.

One of Gabby's children sleeping with Rusty the rescue dog

A couple weeks later, Rusty showed his **devotion** to his new family. Gabby and her kids were napping. Suddenly, Rusty started **pacing** and barking. "He jumped up and started tugging at my sleeve," Gabby said. "He just wouldn't stop." She knew something was wrong.

Dogs bark for many reasons. They bark to show excitement, fear, and other emotions. Dogs also bark to get their owners' attention.

"When I opened the door, smoke filled the hallway," Gabby said. She picked up her kids and ran outside with Rusty. Gabby raced back inside to get the family cat. That's when she saw the small fire in her kitchen. Gabby grabbed a **fire extinguisher** and put it out.

The fire was caused by a faulty outlet in the kitchen.

If it wasn't for Rusty, Gabby and her family might not have escaped the fire. "It's almost as if he was meant to come into our lives and meant . . . to save us," she said. Now, Gabby feels an even stronger connection to her special dog. Rusty, who was rescued himself, is now a rescuer.

Rusty the hero dog, shown here, is an important part of Gabby's family.

Hero Dog Ella

Ella the **Labrador** is also a dog hero. But she saved her family from a different threat. It was the summer of 2022 in Utah. The Michaelis family was swimming in their pool. They had no idea danger was **lurking** nearby—that is, until Ella, the family dog, began acting strange.

The Michaelis family often spent summer days in their backyard pool.

Instead of playing, Ella stood on a rock wall near the pool. "She kept looking at the kids and then quickly looking back," said Crystal Michaelis, the children's mom. "My daughter thought it was very concerning."

The Michaelis family lives in Pleasant Grove, Utah. Their home is surrounded by mountains.

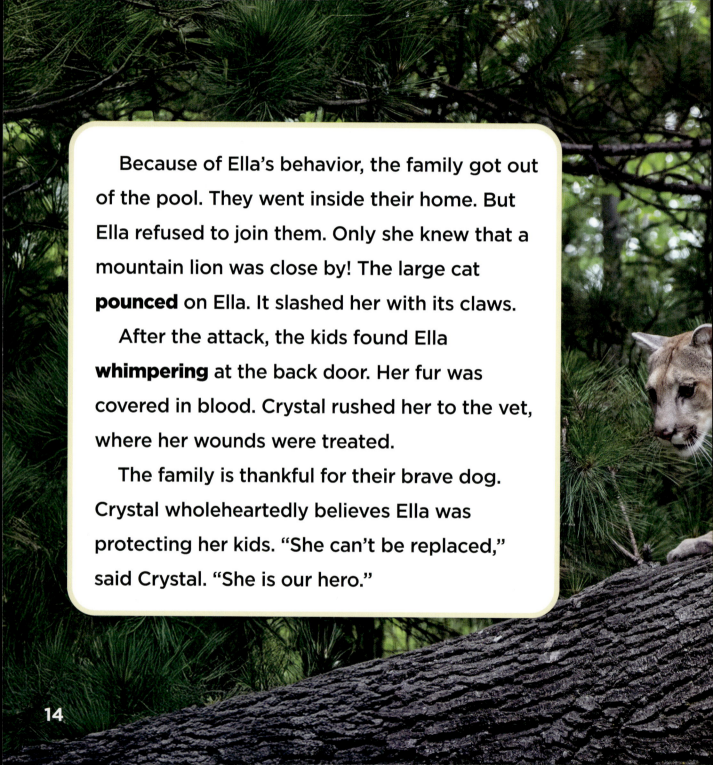

Because of Ella's behavior, the family got out of the pool. They went inside their home. But Ella refused to join them. Only she knew that a mountain lion was close by! The large cat **pounced** on Ella. It slashed her with its claws.

After the attack, the kids found Ella **whimpering** at the back door. Her fur was covered in blood. Crystal rushed her to the vet, where her wounds were treated.

The family is thankful for their brave dog. Crystal wholeheartedly believes Ella was protecting her kids. "She can't be replaced," said Crystal. "She is our hero."

Mountain lions have razor-sharp claws. They use their claws to climb and catch prey.

15

Sarah Saves the Day

Dog heroes come in all sizes. Sarah Jane, a beagle mix, is a small dog with a loud bark. In 2022, Harry Smith, Sarah's owner, was taking her for a walk. That's when the unthinkable happened. Harry lost control of the electric wheelchair he uses. The left wheel of the chair "grabbed and spun me," said Harry. He rolled down a bank into a lake. Harry struggled to keep his head above water. He was afraid he might drown.

Dogs like Sarah Jane are very helpful to people with disabilities. They can help keep them safe.

Luckily, Sarah knew exactly what to do. She barked for help. The little dog barked so loudly that people came running. One person flagged down a police officer. He and the others pulled Harry from the water. Harry's wheelchair was destroyed. But thankfully, he was fine.

Harry will never forget that day as long as he lives. When asked about Sarah, Harry said, she is my "hero." He also said, "I love her. Always have, always will."

Beagles are known for their loud yodel-like bark. This special bark is called a bay.

Tater Tot and Tom

Tater Tot, a three-legged Pomeranian mix, is an even smaller lifesaver. He's the beloved pet of Tom Kissel. One day, Tom was walking Tater on a dock near a lake. All of a sudden, waves from a big boat rocked the dock. Both Tom and his little dog **plunged** into the water.

As Tom fell, he hit his head on the dock and sank underwater. Tater swam **frantically** around him. A woman saw the little dog and ran over. She and her husband grabbed Tom and pulled him to safety. They believe if Tater hadn't stayed with Tom, he would have drowned.

After the scary **ordeal**, Tom hugged Tater. "Thank you for saving me," he said. "I couldn't ask for a better friend."

Pomeranians are small dogs with big personalities.

PROFILE:
Dog Rescuers

Why do some dogs rescue and protect people? Here are some amazing dog qualities that could explain why.

Loyal
Dogs form strong bonds with their owners. They will guard and protect people they know as well as seek comfort from them.

Social
Dogs are pack animals. They prefer the company of other dogs and people, who they often consider to be members of their pack.

Intelligent
The average dog can learn up to 165 words! Experts say most dogs are as smart as a toddler.

Glossary

adopted (uh-DOPT-uhd)
taken into one's family

devotion (dih-VOH-shuhn)
love or loyalty for something

fire extinguisher (FYE-ur ek-STING-gwish-ur)
a device that releases chemicals to put out a fire

frantically (FRAN-tik-lee)
to do something with worry or fear

Labrador (LAB-ruh-dor)
a breed of dog with short, thick black, brown, or yellow fur

lurking (LURK-ing)
secretly hiding

ordeal (or-DEEL)
a difficult experience

pacing (PAYSS-ing)
anxiously walking back and forth

plunged (PLUHNJD)
fell quickly into

pounced (POUNST)
jumped onto something suddenly

shelter (SHEL-tur)
a place that houses homeless or lost animals

volunteered (vol-uhn-TEERD)
contributed one's time to help others for no pay

whimpering (WIM-pur-ing)
making a crying sound

Find Out More

BOOKS

Markovics, Joyce. *Amazing Animal Minds: Dogs*. Ann Arbor, MI: Cherry Lake Press, 2024.

Markovics, Joyce. *Champs! Inspirational Animals: Fearless Dogs*. Ann Arbor, MI: Cherry Lake Press, 2024.

Recio, Belinda. *When Animals Rescue*. New York, NY: Skyhorse Publishing, 2021.

WEBSITES

Explore these online sources with an adult:

Britannica Kids: Dog

National Geographic Kids: Dog Facts for Kids!

University of Michigan Critter Catalog: Dogs

Index

accident, 16, 20
adoption, animal, 7
animal shelter, 6
Bannon, Gabby, 4–11
barking, 9, 18–19
children, 8, 13–14
Ella the dog, 12–15
fire, 10–11
fire extinguisher, 10
Hurricane Helene, 4–5
Kissel, Tom, 20
Labrador, 12
lake, 16, 20
mountain lion, 14–15
North Carolina, 4–6
Pennsylvania, 4, 7
police officer, 18
Rusty the dog, 6–11
Sarah Jane the dog, 16–18
Smith, Harry, 16–18
Tater Tot the dog, 20
Utah, 12–13
volunteers, 4, 6
wheelchair, 16–18

About the Author

Joyce Markovics is drawn to stories that tug at her heart. When she's not writing books for kids, she volunteers at an animal sanctuary where dozens of different species peacefully coexist. Joyce would like to thank Gabby Bannon for her generous contribution to this book.